D1583771

PEEPS INTO
GARSTANG'S PAST

by

DENIS TETLOW

Table of Contents

Author's Note

When Garstang Heritage Society was formed in 1981, one of its aims was to produce, in due course, a History of Garstang. This has not yet materialized.

I have spent many hours in the Lancashire Record Office and have obtained a lot of information about the town, mainly from the minute books of various organisations. Unfortunately, these only cover the 19th and 20th centuries. There is little obvious information relating to earlier years.

Although the information that I have unearthed does not constitute a complete history of Garstang, I have summarized it in this short book rather than let the information that I have be lost. I hope that it will be of general interest and perhaps stimulate someone with the appropriate skills to produce a more complete history of the town.

Denis Tetlow

Sources

Lancashire Record Office:

Minute Books of Local Government Bodies
Record Book re Garstang Corporation
Record Book of Garstang Friendly Society

Norfolk Record Office:

Keppel Rent Roll of 1842

Hewitson, A (Atticus),
Our Country Chapels and Churches, 1890

Acknowledgements

W N Bamber, Peter Frankental, Audrey Tetlow,
Helen Tetlow
(typing and proof-reading)

Derek Reay (assembly of photographs)

Kathleen Kenning (front cover design)

Printed March, 2001

Important Dates in the History of Garstang

A.D.1000

c1150- William de Lancastre - Lord of the Manor of
1246   Garstang. (3 generations - all called William)

1226   Fulling Mill at Garstang conveyed to Richard de Boteller

1246   Garstang Manor demised to Abbot of Cockersand

1314   Edward II gave the Abbot of Cockersand the right to hold a weekly market in Garstang

1332   Town raided by Scots

1359   Town ravaged by plague

1437   Mention of Chapel of Ease in Garstang (believed to be on land just to rear of where Market Hall stands)

1490   Greenhalgh Castle built by the 1st Earl of Derby (4 towers 14 yds by 16 yds)
Probably first stone bridge over the River Wyre, near the Mill, built at this time

1540   Dissolution of the Monasteries. Manor of Garstang reverted to the Crown
Probably no weekly market for next 50 years

1590   Mill House cottage built

1597   Elizabeth 1 granted right to hold a Weekly Market and two Annual Fairs

1602   School opened in Churchtown

1627   Wyre Bridge rebuilt

1644   Greenhalgh Castle besieged for 12 months by Commonwealth troops

1649   Greenhalgh Castle demolished

1666   Chapel of Ease rebuilt

1680	August 5th Charles II gave Town a Charter. Town Hall probably built at this time
1715	Scottish Insurgents passed through the town. 4 of the local men who joined them subsequently hanged. (1 in Preston, 3 locally)
1750	Town Hall destroyed by fire (Town Records lost) Wyre Bridge rebuilt
1751	Sir Edward Walpole became owner of the Manor of Garstang. He passed title to his daughter when she married a Keppel
1754	A Market Cross removed. This probably stood on land in front of the site of the Kings Arms
1755	Town Hall rebuilt
1756	Grammar School built
1770	St Thomas' Chapel built on present site
1777	Congregational Church built
1788	First Catholic Church built on land off Back Lane – later to become The Institute
1797	Preston-Kendal Canal opened
1814	First Wesleyan Chapel built on present site
1815	Vestry appointed Committee of 12 people to look after the poor
1820	Oil lamps placed at street corners
1829	Wyre Bridge widened
1833	"Water Witch" express service Kendal to Preston 7 hours each way, 114 miles in 15 hours, 2 horses changed every 4 miles
1834	Poor Law Unions set up
1843	Market Hall built
1844	St Thomas' school built
1856	Police Station built
1858	Catholic Church and School built in Bonds

1860　First Post Office at Wrightson's Printers in High
　　　 Street
1867　Auction of Manor of Garstang in London - (with
　　　 drawn - bids only £70-£80,000)
1870　Garstang – Pilling Railway opened
　　　 Railway closed 1872-75 because engine worn out
1872　Sanitary Authority formed
1873　First piped water in town
1874　New Workhouse built in Bonds - cost £6,000
　　　 Average 34 inmates
1875　Railway re-opened following purchase of new
　　　 engine (Pilling Pig)
1878　Mr Storey lit town for £10/10/- (Oil lamps)
1880　Gas works opened in Kepple Lane
　　　 Gas Works lit town - 14 lights for £17/10/- 10th
　　　 October to 31st March
1881　G Boys Stones became first Vicar of Garstang
1882　Stoops Hall rebuilt by Collinsons
　　　 Wesleyan Church rebuilt (£1,650) and Manse on
　　　 Bowgreave (£1,219/19/8)
　　　 New Surface Drain and Sewer along High Street,
　　　 Church Street to Smithspool
1883　Municipal Corporations Act – replaced Bailiff and
　　　 Burgesses with Rural District Council.
　　　 First Scavenger (Street Sweeper) appointed –
　　　 £4 for 6 months
1889　Town Trust formed
　　　 Liberal Club opened
1893　Institute enlarged
　　　 Petty Sessions moved from Town Hall to Institute
1894　Local Government Act - Parish Council replaced
　　　 Vestry

1897	Market Cross renovated. (2 side-lamps replaced, 1 lamp on top)
1900	Railway extended to Knott End
1912	Guardian Union Buildings built
1919	First 'Democratic' Election of Parish Councillors
1920	First bus services Garstang – Preston
1925	Library opened in Institute – 1 night per week
1928	Grammar School closed
1930	Passenger Traffic ceased on Railway

Lords of the Manor

In 1246 William de Lancastre demised the place now called Garstang, with some land, to the Abbey of Cockersand.

The property reverted to the Crown in 1540, at the time of the dissolution of the monasteries by Henry VIII. During the next 200 years the Manor of Garstang passed through various hands under a lease created by the Crown. The lease expired in 1738 and a new one was created in 1742 for a period of 31 years. This was assigned to Hon Edward Walpole in 1751 who was given a new 31-year lease. Subsequently, Walpole made a representation to the King advising that Garstang was a market town situated on the common highway from London to the West of Scotland. Its status as a staging post meant that any improvement to the town would be of public benefit and serve to encourage trade and manufacturing in and about the town. However, as Walpole only possessed a relatively short lease, it was not in his interest to invest capital in the place. The upshot of this was that an Act of Parliament was passed enabling the King to sell the Manor of Garstang to Walpole. Walpole gave the Manor to one of his daughters when she married into the Keppel family, whose home was in Norfolk.

For the next 165 years Garstang was owned by the Keppel family. They were absentee landlords. They did try to sell the town "en bloc" in 1867 at an auction in London but the reserve price (believed to be between £70-80,000) was not reached. Subsequently many of the properties were sold off piecemeal and in November 1919 the remainder were sold at an auction held in Garstang.

The Development of Garstang

The development of Garstang is a matter of fact, but the precise nature of its early development leaves much to conjecture.

In 1226 William de Boteller became owner of a Fulling Mill on the River Wyre at Garstang. At that time the wild moss land would not have been far away from the west bank of the river and the Forest of Bowland would have pressed down upon its eastern bank. There would probably have been a small group of wood and thatch buildings on the high ground on the west side of the river, the present Market Place, where the millworkers lived. Even in those days the track which was the embryo A6 passed this way, crossing the river either by stepping stones or a wooden bridge, and the wives of the mill-workers would be glad to earn a little by providing food and shelter at this half-way spot for travellers between Preston and Lancaster.

Three generations, all called William de Lancaster, owned the town, which they leased over the years to a variety of tenants, but there was probably little development until the Abbot of Cockersand became Lord of the Manor of Garstang in 1246. Even then growth would probably have been slow until Edward II gave the town in 1314 the right to hold a weekly market. This would have brought dwellers in neighbouring villages and hamlets into the town and encouraged the Abbots to build more properties so as to provide shops and hostelries to meet the growing need.

In 1540 the Crown ordered the dissolution of the monasteries. It was then that Cockersand forfeited the Manor of Garstang, which reverted to the Crown. It is probable that the town would have reached the size at which it would stay for the next 400 years. Rebuilding of properties would of course take place during that period, but the main street of the town would stretch from the river, along Bridge Street, Market Place and High Street as far as Croston Weind. This was a narrow lane with a quite considerable copse of trees at its western end until the beginning of the 20th century. Chapel (now Church) Street would run from the Market Place with properties on the right hand side to just beyond the Farmers Arms. A narrow entry would lead off Church Street into a lane, known as Back Lane, which linked up with Croston Weind. The several Weinds joining High Street and Back Lane contained houses, workshops and outbuildings belonging to the hostelries.

An attractive feature of the town in mediaeval times would have been Smithspool Stream. This flowed from a spot near where Hereford Avenue now stands, running through the fields and crossing Back Lane on the south side of the Wheatsheaf Hotel, then running parallel with the west side of Bridge Street and entering the river by the bridge. The stream became very polluted during the 19th Century and was eventually culverted in the 1890ís.

Dominating the town from 1490 for 150 years was Greenhalgh Castle. Built by Thomas, Earl of Derby, it had four towers with 14 yards between them on two sides and

16 yards between them on the other two. During the Civil War it was held for the King and withstood a siege for twelve months, only surrendering when Captain Anderson, the officer commanding the castle, died. The castle was destroyed by the Commonwealth troops. At the same time as the Earl had built the castle he had also built the first stone bridge over the river. It is said to have been quite narrow and had a watch tower at the northern end from which there could be communication with the castle. The bridge was rebuilt in 1627 and again 1750 and widened in 1829.

The Town in 1842

A Rent Roll relating to the properties belonging to the Manor drawn up in 1842 gives an interesting picture of the town at that time.

It appears obvious that a gradual rebuilding of properties had taken place down the years and Garstang must have had a very chequered appearance. 43 houses were built of stone and slate, 83 of stone and thatch, 21 of brick and thatch and 12 of brick and slate. One building in Back Lane, a nail-maker's shop, was built of mud and thatch. The High Street had a good mix. The east side had 14 stone and slate, 21 stone and thatch, 6 brick and thatch and 4 brick and slate buildings. The west side had 11, 18, 12 and 7 respectively. The Kings Arms is described as a new inn.

Shops in the town included; 6 shoemakers, 4 grocers, 3 butchers, 3 drapers, 3 crockery, 2 plumbers, 2 hatters, 2 ironmongers, 2 saddlers, 1 bonnet, 1 hairdresser, 1 nailor, 1 cabinet-maker, 1 cooper, 1 printer, 1 smithy and 1 rope-walk. The thirty-five outlets at that time compare with approximately 100 in the year 2000, including estate agents, banks and also 3 supermarkets.

There were 4 doctors, 4 lawyers, 1 vet and 13 publicans. The number of persons living in properties owned by the Manor was approximately 600, of whom 263 were children under 14. There were 17 families with five or more children under 14.

Hostelries

The description of some of the hostelries is interesting.

The Royal Oak

The Royal Oak, a Posting Inn, was a stone and slate building containing: tap room, parlour bar, dining room, stone room, kitchen, scullery and a large new room. It had a water closet, 11 bedrooms and 3 servants' rooms. There was a large range of cellars, a spirit room, pantry and washhouse. Various outbuildings contained stabling for 24 horses, some with lofts above. There was a 2-coach house, a brewhouse, pigsties, a cart shed and a "Necessary". The Royal Oak Field extended from the rear of the Hotel westwards as far as the Church and was bounded by the river to the south. The tenant, John Dobson, paid an annual rent of £55/6/-.

The Eagle & Child

The other Posting Inn was the Eagle and Child, let to Joseph Rooking at £43/18/- per annum. Built of stone and slate, it contained 3 parlours, a large market room, a kitchen, back kitchen, pantry and ale cellar. It had 8 bedrooms together with stabling in various outbuildings for 21 horses and 7 beasts. There was also a brewhouse.

The Kings Arms

The Kings Arms, described as a new building of stone and slate with a brick back, contained a parlour and kitchen, a bar parlour, 4 chambers and 2 attics. Outbuildings of brick and thatch contained a brewhouse and stabling for 7 horses. There was a stone and slate building containing

15

pigsties and a shippon for 4 cows. There was also a small garden.

The Pack Horse Inn

The Pack Horse Inn was situated in the block on the east side of the High Street, currently the site of Conway Cards and Billingtons. It was built of brick and thatch and the tenant, William Dunderdale, paid an annual rent of £52/10/-. It contained a large kitchen over which was a newly constructed large room of stone and slate. There were 4 other ground-floor rooms and 5 bedrooms. Outbuildings consisted of stabling for 29 horses including stallion houses, a shippon for 5 cows and a brewhouse. At the rear was a croft in excess of 1 acre, which was a garden and bowling green. It was well known as a place where stallions and mares were brought together for mating.

The Pack Horse lost its licence in 1902 and became a Temperance Hotel. A local resident whose grandmother ran the hotel after 1902 remembered the large kitchen with a long table covered with lovely white cloths where coach parties, before and after the first World War, were given memorable meals. The property was redeveloped after the 1914-18 War.

The Golden Ball

The Golden Ball public house was situated on the site in Bridge Street currently occupied by B & S Supplies. The slight incline of Bridge Street to the Market Place was known as Ball Brow. Built of stone and thatch it contained 3 parlours, a taproom, kitchen, pantry and cellar, a first floor 'club room' and 4 bedrooms. It had about 1/2 acre of pastureland and a large garden. It also had stabling for 5 horses, a shippon for 4 cows, a pigsty and a brewhouse. It closed in 1925.

Other Hostelries

Of the other 8 hostelries in the town, 3 were in Church Street. Nearest the Market Place was the Horns Inn, so called because of a magnificent set of antlers over the door. The Brown Cow, one of the oldest pubs in the town dating from 1685, was on a site in Church Street backing on to the Methodist Church. It closed as a pub towards the end of the 19th Century and became a cake shop. It was demolished in 1930. The Shovel & Broom (now the Farmers Arms) had a large clubroom over the stabling. Like all the other pubs it had a brewhouse and pigsties. It also had a large garden and yard where a fair was held on Fair Days.

The Wheatsheaf on Back Lane, built of brick, stone and thatch, also had a large clubroom. A stone and slate building containing a storeroom and stabling for 8 horses had recently been built. When the cattle sale took place in the town in November it was customary for sheep to be sold at the front of the Wheatsheaf.

The other four pubs were all on the High Street at the northern end. The Swan, was rebuilt as the Crown in 1911. The new building was slightly to the north and east of the previous site. The Blue Anchor was roughly on the site of the present Co-op Supermarket. The Red Lion was situated where The Flower Shop currently stands. Both were apparently cottage properties but had quite substantial outbuildings including the usual brewhouses, pigsties and shippons. They both closed well before the end of the 19th Century. Before the cottages were demolished, the one which had been the Blue Anchor became Garstang's first fish and chip shop in the early years of the 20th Century.

The other High Street pub was situated in the premises now known as Laburnum Cottage, which was built in 1850. The pub was generally known as the Holy Lamb, but in the rent roll it is called The Fleece Inn and is described as a miserable dilapidated building. That is probably why it was rebuilt in 1850. Here again quite extensive outbuildings are described, obviously running down towards Back Lane.

The other pub worth a mention is not in Garstang but in Bonds. Currently called the Church Inn, it was there before the Catholic Church was built and was then known as the Rose and Crown. There really seems little need of another pub so near to Garstang. It has been suggested that this was possibly opened at the end of the 18th Century to meet the needs of the canal navvies who apparently did not like drinking with the locals and vice versa.

It would appear that the hostelries with their many outbuildings and gardens must have occupied well over a quarter of the area covered by the town.

19th Century Garstang

Hostelries

Why were there so many hostelries in the town? The population varied during the 19th Century between 687 and 929. It was highest during the first half of that period. A population of 900 suggests an adult male total of 200 – 250, an average of about 17 for each pub. The large number of hostelries is indicative of how much passing trade Garstang must have had in the first half of the 19th Century to support so many pubs. Of course there was no clean tap water, no cafes, no take-aways available, so anyone needing a drink or a meal would have to go into a pub.

Every day in 1824 eight coaches called at the Royal Oak, four going north and four south. The last one to the north left at midnight. Two coaches to the north and two to the south stopped at the Eagle and Child. There must have been numerous visitors from surrounding villages and the big houses particularly on market day, and one can imagine the main streets being very busy, not only with pedestrians but also with horses with or without carriages.

Stables

Although there appears to have been plenty of stabling in the town this was not sufficient to meet the needs. A large stable block called Rochdale House with accommodation for ostlers was built at the northwest corner of the junction of Lancaster Road and Green Lane. This is marked on the

Ordnance Survey Map of 1847 but has disappeared by 1893. There must have been a steady movement of horses from the town centre to Rochdale House and back.

Roads

It is interesting to note that Lancaster Road was often referred to as Scotland Road or London Road depending upon whether one was travelling north or south. This stretch of road has another reason to be remembered. On the O.S. Map of 1847 a lane is shown leaving the west side of the road at the place where currently a path goes to Oak Road Community Primary School. The lane was called Hanging Lane and on a Field Map of 1842 the small field on the southwest side of the junction of these roads was called Gallows Field. In the 19th Century there was a belief in the town that three of the four local rebels who joined the Old Pretender's army in 1715 were hung about half a mile to the north of the town and not in Catterall as was generally supposed. This lane and field would seem to validate their belief. The lane had disappeared by 1893. Another point worth noting is that Wyre Lane used to be called Ridge Lane.

The main roads of the town would most probably be sur- faced with crushed limestone with cobbled sidewalks. Atticus (the pseudonym of A. Hewitson, author of 'Our Country Chapels and Churches' 1890) reported that unless your shoes had soles 2 inches thick, it was a torture to walk down the streets. There are frequent appeals in the various Minute Books for the water cart to be used more frequently to lay the dust in summer. In wet weather potholes would be full of water and the streets would bear witness to the passage of many horses. These droppings would be added to by the daily passage of cows moving from the small farm situated behind the Swan Hotel (now the Crown) to pasture off Moss Lane.

Waste disposal
Night soil was collected and deposited in large holes in fields off Kepple Lane. In the 19th Century Kepple Lane was called Kettle Lane. A kettle was a hollow in the ground gouged out during the Ice Age. The fields in Kettle Lane were called: Big Kettle, Middle Kettle etc. When you consider that all the inns brewed their own beer and kept their own pigs, and that the four butchers had their own slaughter houses which had few hygiene regulations until late in the 19th century, then on a warm damp day with a breeze blowing from the south-west, Garstang residents must not have breathed too deeply.

Canal transport
The opening of the Kendal to Preston Canal in 1797 brought the first challenge to horse-drawn transport. It was built to enable coal to be carried from the Lancashire coalfields to Cumberland and for limestone to be brought south for road making. During the 60 years until the railways were established it was very profitable. 617,000 tons of goods were carried in the peak year of 1840. It also had a good passenger service. In 1833 a boat called the 'Water Witch' covered the journey from Kendal to Preston and back, a distance of 114 miles, in 15 hours. The boat was pulled by two horses which were changed every four

miles. The average speed was 10 mph. The fare from Lancaster to Preston was 3/- (1st class) and 2/- (2nd class). The Lancaster Guardian (24.11.1928) reported that 16,000 passengers used the service in the first six months. The canal was leased to Lancaster & Preston Railway for 21 years from 1842; the lease was transferred to Lancaster & Carlisle Railway in 1849.

The railway

The main line railway station for Garstang was situated 2 – 3 miles out of the town near the Kenlis Arms. A branch line connecting the main line with Garstang and Pilling was opened in 1870. The company had only one engine. It made nine journeys a day from Garstang Town Station to the main line and three journeys a day to Pilling and back. There were no trains on Sundays. In 1872 the engine stopped, worn out, and the line closed till 1875 when a new engine, called the Farmers Friend, later the Pilling Pig, was hired. The line was extended to Knott End in 1908. In 1919 the company was taken over by the LMS (London, Midland & Scotland) Railway.

Employment

The canal and the railway slowly brought an end to the stagecoach traffic and must have affected the prosperity of the town. The population fell from 929 in 1831 to 687 in 1871 as people left to find jobs in the growing industrial towns. Numbers could well have fallen further had it not been for the establishment at Nateby in 1850 of the business of Collinson's. The main interest of the business was building agricultural machinery but it expanded to undertake building work, laying of drains, general contracting work and even had a funeral service. At its peak before the 1914-18 War the firm employed 137 people and many of Garstang's skilled workers served their apprenticeship with Collinson's. The firm appears to have been unwilling to move into the mechanised age and in 1929 the business was wound up.

Another business which served the "horse age" was Harrison's Saddlery firm which operated in Church Street behind the Royal Oak before the 1914-18 War. It employed 13 people. The son of the owner, while serving in the army in France, saw the introduction of tanks and lorries and realised that the future of the horse was limited. When he came home he purchased the hardware business of a man called Smith operating in a building on the site where the present Harrison's hardware shop is situated.

On the land which is now the site of Booth's car park there were a number of allotment gardens worked by people living on the High Street. Adjacent to these on the north side was the long ropewalk. (This was situated on the west side of Back Lane approximately on the site of the road now called Rope Walk. The rope was made in a long row of stone and thatched buildings which covered about 60 feet.) The grounds of both the Eagle and Child and King's Arms extended across what is now Park Hill Road. The northern end of the land now occupied by Nickson's DIY Store was the site of Garstang's first cattle auction, which moved in 1923 to its new site in Claughton.

Entertainment

The centre of outdoor entertainment before the 1939-45 War was the Royal Oak Field. This very large field stretched westward from the back of the Royal Oak to St Thomas' Church and in a southerly direction as far as the river. It was the site of the Whitsuntide Festival, the Agricultural Show, Circus events and all other outdoor celebrations. Boating on the river from the mill up as far as Hippingstones was a popular summer pastime. There was a cricket ground, initially on a field in Moss Lane, just beyond what was the Gas Works. The venue was moved in 1912 to a field off Lancaster Road, now part of the flood barrier. A tennis club occupied a site across the river in Bonds.

On Shrove Tuesday at 11 am the Market Bell was rung, school finished for the day and apprentices also left work. The youngsters ranged around the town begging at doors, receiving sweets or pancakes, and scrambling to pick up hot pennies thrown by various publicans. (Hot pennies were pennies which had been heated in a shovel on a fire before being scattered. This was the publicans' way of adding a little "fun" and a few burnt fingers to the proceedings!).

On Easter Monday, many children joined in the practice of 'pace egging', dozens of multi-coloured hard-boiled eggs being rolled down the slope of Broom Hill, the small hill encountered after turning left over Hippingstones Ford at the end of Wyre Lane.

The big event of the year was the Whit Festival procession and sports. Before the 1914 -18 War the Catholics and Protestants held separate functions both preceded by a church service. The Catholics celebrated on a field in Bonds and the Protestants on the Royal Oak Field, following processions round the town. After the 1914 -18 War the processions were combined and the church services discontinued. The daytime celebrations were followed by a dance, which generally lasted until the early hours of the morning.

The Agricultural Show on the Royal Oak Field was another long awaited day and was a hive of activity. There was also a Fair in the yard of the Farmers Arms. The Show was wound up after a long night on the dance floor.

The Cattle and Horse Fair

The other great outdoor activity in the town took place on two days at the end of November. On the first day cattle were sold and on the next day there was a horse fair. Shop fronts were boarded up as hundreds of cattle, many from Scotland and Ireland thronged the streets. Boys were paid to guard groups of cattle while their owners were in the pubs. On the day of the horse sales the animals would show off their paces galloping up and down the High Street. After the Great War the attendance at the fairs fell rapidly and the last fair was held in 1932. A report in the Lancashire Daily Post in November 1933 states that no fair was held but gives a graphic report of its past glories:

"The older people of Garstang retain vivid memories of past November Fairs and recall times when many thousands of cattle were collected. Imagine 6,000 beasts in possession of Garstang's quaint old streets and weinds. Small wonder barricades were erected to protect property. For the week the Fair lasted the whole neighbourhood made it a holiday. Every pub had a dancing room and revelry went on until the early hours. Landlords hoped to make a year's rent while the Fair lasted. Roundabouts, hobby horses, coconut shies and travelling museums filled the town. This was the area's one yearly holiday. It was from this Fair that the farmers replenished their cattle stocks and no other Fair in the north country attained quite so high a status as Garstang".

In different records all sorts of figures between 2,000 and 20,000 are mentioned as the number of cattle at the Fair. Just how many cows would fit into Garstang's streets? What a mess the streets and the floors of the pubs must have been, particularly if the weather was wet!

Entertainment venues

Apart from the pubs, places for indoor entertainment were a bit limited until the mid-nineteenth century. The only reasonable room for a concert or dance was in the Town Hall. However, after the Catholic Church moved to Bonds in 1858, their premises off Back Lane eventually became a Reading Room and Entertainment Centre known as the Institute. These premises were sold by the Keppel family to the Trustees of the Institute in 1870.

In 1882 there was a great controversy over the use of the

Centre. At that time the Trustees of the property were in the main staunch Tories while the Management Committee had strong Liberal leanings. In May 1882 the Liberals booked the room for a political meeting. The Trustees were outraged because they said that there was an unwritten agreement that the premises would not be used for religious or political meetings. To stop the meeting from being held on the day of the event the Trustees barricaded the premises and the meeting had to be held in the Town Hall. The vitriolic correspondence between Tories and Liberals published in the Lancaster press over the following weeks has to be read to be believed.

One outcome of this was the decision of the Liberals to build their own premises and these were opened in Bridge Street on 19th February 1899 with a great deal of pomp and ceremony. Besides a Reading Room and Billiard Room on the ground floor, there was a large Ballroom on the first floor. This became known as the Assembly Room to avoid any political taint. It was a very popular location for the annual dances of many organisations. Before the 1914 -18 War it was also the venue of a weekly "hop". Men paid 3d to attend. Ladies went in free.

Following the opening of the Liberal Club, the Institute was enlarged in 1893, a Billiard Room, Games Room and Kitchen being added. Later in its history it was to be the home of moving pictures in the town.

Churches

The Anglican Church (St Thomas)

A chapel in Gayrestang in 1326 is mentioned in some deeds of the Dalton family of Thurnham. It is believed this chapel was situated on land to the rear of Carrick House on the High Street. The mother church was St Helen's in Churchtown. There is an interesting booklet written by Rev W B Porteus detailing the development of St Thomas' Church. Briefly, the old chapel was described in 1769 as being in a decayed condition. The site of the old chapel was too small to contain a new church of the size required. In 1770 a new church was built on its present site in Church Street. Anyone who subscribed £20 or more towards the cost of the new church building was guaranteed a double seat in the front part of the church and a bench for servants. Thirty-eight people subscribed. The building cost £546/9/1½d. Various alterations have taken place to the premises down the years.

The Catholic Church

Following the Dissolution of 1540, Catholics in Garstang had no place to worship. The Keppel family were staunch members of the Church of England and would not sell land in Garstang to the Catholics, who were forced to travel to either Claughton or Scorton to worship. However, in 1785 a Mr Horrabin who lived in the house in the High Street that has for many years been a chemist's shop, leased the bottom part of his garden, which ran down to Back Lane, to the Catholic community. A church which could hold 500 people was erected as well as a small house for the priest. A history of the Catholic Church in Garstang written by Mr R N Bamber gives a full and interesting account of developments. Suffice it to say that the church on Back Lane became too small and after an interesting struggle the incumbent priest, Father Hickey, managed to acquire in 1856 the land in Bonds on which the present church and school stand. It is interesting to note that Father Hickey was the priest from 1825 to 1871, a period when there was not much love lost between Protestants and Catholics. However, it was reported that his funeral was attended by people of all denominations in the town.

Free churches

Garstang Independent Chapel was built in 1777 on Croston Weind. Many of its original congregation were the Scottish servants of the Duke of Hamilton who lived at Woodacre Hall. The minister for many years, up to 1825, was a Mr Grimshaw who, it was reported, claimed the biggest congregation in the town. After he died there was apparently a change of emphasis in the form of worship and a portion of the congregation split away and formed the Particular Baptist Church in Nateby. The Sunday School was built in 1904.

The first Methodist (then Wesleyan) Chapel was built in 1814 on its present site. Before the chapel was built open-air services in front of the Royal Oak were occasionally held in summer and a room on the first floor of a shop in Stoops Hall was rented. The present chapel was built in 1879.

A Meeting House of Friends (Quakers) was built in 1830 in a delightful setting on land given to the Friends by Richard Jackson, himself a Quaker. This land was at the rear of his big house in Calder House Lane. The Meeting flourished in the 19th Century and after almost disappearing is now again an active Meeting.

Schools

The first school building in the area was erected in Churchtown in 1602 on a site opposite the present School. In the early years of the 19th century it was the best attended school in the district. The headmaster at the time was a John Cornthwaite. It is reported that his peculiarity was his earnestness and his passion for flogging lads. The school's popularity diminished towards the end of the century.

In the Lancashire Records Office there is an undated list of schools in Garstang. From the population figures quoted the year may have been 1831. The Grammar School had 45 males and 10 females. The Roman Catholic School had 30 children paid for by the Church and 35 paying scholars. There were two other schools; one for children of either sex paid for by their parents, the other commenced in 1826 with about the same number of pupils. No details of these schools are given.

The Grammar School
The Keppels leased a plot of land to the town in 1756 at an annual rent of 2/6d on which a school was to be built. John Morland of Winmarleigh endowed the school with £150. This latter sum was used by the Bailiff to pay off a town debt but an allowance of £6/15/- per annum was to be made to pay the schoolmaster. Four boys selected by the Bailiff received free tuition. The salary increased very slowly over the years reaching £10 in 1817. It remained at that figure until 1876 when the school was placed under

the Government Inspection. The salary was then increased to £20 plus a Government grant. (£5 had to be spent on the school). The headmaster's income was augmented by the receipt of school pence. These were small payments made by parents/ guardians at many schools until free education was introduced.

The above-mentioned list of schools shows that there were girls attending this school but there is no mention of a schoolmistress being appointed. Tradition has it that the girls were taught on a gallery in the schoolroom. There is little reported in the Corporation Records until 1844 when the Curate of Garstang Chapel, Rev W Armistead, wrote to the Bailiff requesting that the Corporation remove the existing headmaster, Mr Ebeneezer Wells, on the grounds of his unfitness for the situation. He also requested that they should appoint in his place some person who had received training at the Chester Training College, and that the Trustees should permit the Rev Armistead to aid in the religious instruction of the scholars.

The Bailiff replied that the request had been considered but they refused to do as suggested, and added that the Protestant clergymen of the town would be at perfect liberty to visit the school, subject to such conditions as the Trustees might think fit to prescribe.

Between 1858-1877 the school had seven headmasters. This lack of continuity may have caused the place to deteriorate. In 1872 Atticus (the pseudonym used by A Hewitson, author of *Our Country Chapels and Churches*

1890) reports looking into the building. He said the interior was dirty and slovenly, there were a few old dingy maps on the wall and a wicked-looking comb hanging by a piece of string near the door.

There were books here and there, book leaves strewn on the floor and a lot of odds and ends in a careless condition, tempting one to believe that somebody had been having a fight and run away believing the police were coming.

In 1880 some continuity arrived with the appointment of R B Winchester as headmaster who stayed until 1898. Mr Joseph Irvine, who then became headmaster, remained until the school closed in 1928 and under his guidance the place achieved a good academic and sporting standard. With the increasing accessibility of other schools in Preston and Lancaster the numbers at the Grammar School fell and eventually Lancashire County Council decided it should close.

The Catholic School
The Catholic School is believed to have been opened in 1800. There is some doubt as to where the school was situated, but the Rent Roll of 1842 places it between Moss Lane Barn Cottages and the Wheatsheaf Hotel describing it as a large stone and slate building. Before Harrison's present shop was built there was a large stone and slate building on the site, which would most probably have housed the school until the new premises were built in Bonds in 1858.

Other Schools

St Thomas' Day School was erected in 1845 on land given by the Keppel family with the aid of a grant from The National Society for the Promotion of Religious Education in accordance with the principles of the Church of England. Land was acquired for a playground in 1884 and the building was enlarged in 1901.

A Miss James ran a Dame School in her home in Church Street for a good number of years at the beginning of the 20th century. Following its closure around 1911, elderly residents of Garstang report that Dr Roberts who lived at Sion Hill opened a school in his home for the children of Wesleyans. They also report that Mary Thomas held a school for girls in the Congregational Sunday School. They could not remember for how long these facilities were available.

A Garstang Character

The Records make little mention of individuals living in Garstang. However, an undated cutting from the Preston Guardian makes mention of Thomas Noble, a Grocer and Tallow Merchant, who lived in the same house in Church Street, Garstang all his life (1776-1865).

He studied law with a Mr Gardiner of Sion Hill but gave it up saying: *'He could not become a lawyer and serve God'.* However it is said that he probably made more wills than all the lawyers in Preston and Lancaster put together, and that not one was contested.

For Garstang and neighbourhood Mr. Noble was lawyer, legislator and judge. He was unmarried but took charge of his brother's 17 children.

Highways and Tolls

In 1555 under a Highways Act the upkeep of the roads became the responsibility of parishes. Individuals had to provide 4 days labour (6 from 1691) or pay a fine or provide a substitute. This was abolished in 1835. A surveyor (Waywarden) was to be appointed in each parish.

In 1773 the Turnpike Act allowed a stretch of road, under the management of a Trust, to charge tolls to be used to maintain the road. Some turnpike roads were licensed by special Act of Parliament before this date, one such being the road from Preston to Lancaster and thence on to Heiring Syke in Westmorland (1751). A body of Trustees was appointed to control the part of this road between Preston and Garstang.

Toll Houses were erected at Broughton and I quote: "Upon Claughton Moor between the place where the roads to the Market Town and Churchtown divide and the lane leading down to Claughton".

List of Tolls Payable

Coach (of any description) drawn by	4 horses	1/-
-do-	3 horses	6d.
-do-	1 horse	3d.

Unladen wagon	1/-
Wagon carrying any kind of fuel	1/-
Other laden wagon	2/-
Every other sort of unladen cart drawn by 1 animal	1d.

Every horse, mare, gelding, mule or ass	1d.
Cattle	10d. a score
Sheep	5d. a score

The Vicar of Garstang paid a nominal 2d per annum to permit himself or his curate to pass the tollgate. Eventually other people were allowed to take out an annual contract.

In order to facilitate road building, the Surveyor had authority to remove sand, stones and other materials from the grounds of any person through which the road passed. Exemptions were made for gardens and other planted areas of more than 5 years standing.

The Trustees were empowered to borrow money against the income from the Tolls. In 1755 they borrowed £500 but the income was insufficient to repay the loan. Salaries of the Toll House keepers were reduced from £20 to £15 p.a. and no further compounding of the Tolls was permitted for the time being.

Eventually the Trustees passed the collecting of Tolls to individuals. The power to levy tolls was put out to public tender and in 1770 a sum of £350, the best bid received, was paid for this power. In subsequent years bids were lower and for 4 years from 1777 Reuben Cork of Claughton paid £280 p.a. In 1781 this rose to £340.

At this date the minuted records end. An Act of Parliament was passed laying the cost of repairing former turnpike roads on the Highways Board as of January 1871. Garstang Union Highways Board was formed in 1863. To enable the Parish Overseer to assess the amount of local rate he would have to levy for repair work, surveyors were required to give him 6 months notice of the amount of money they estimated would be needed to repair the parish roads during the following 6 months.

The major roads in Garstang were at this time surfaced with crushed limestone. In dry weather they became very dusty and there are many requests in the minuted records for the water cart to be used more frequently to lay the dust.

In 1879 Garstang Gas Works were given authority by the Highways Board to break up the highway as necessary in order to carry gas supplies round the area. During the next 20-30 years the streets were dug up frequently as sewers and drains were laid. In winter there would have been innumerable potholes filled with water.

In January 1892 the cost of breaking up and repairing Garstang High Street was estimated at £207/7/6 and was sent to Lancashire County Council. A minute of 18 August 1892 states briefly that work on remaking Garstang High Street was in progress. Then a further minute on 24th November of that year states that the work on remaking the High Street was "stood over". These minutes are very brief and there is no subsequent reference to this work.

In 1895 the duties of the Highway Board were taken over by Garstang Rural District Council.

Early Forms of Government

It is believed that most of the town records were destroyed in a fire that damaged the Town Hall in 1750. We can assume that while the town belonged to the Abbey at Cockersand, the monks would control the town affairs and it is possible that the first house on the site of Sion Hill may have been built at this time, not only as a home for the monks looking after the town and the mill, but also as a halfway house between Preston and Lancaster where any clerics travelling between monasteries could find accommodation.

The monasteries had always been responsible for the care of the poor within their boundaries, and when they were dissolved in 1540 this responsibility fell upon the local Church, especially where, as in the case of Garstang, the Town was owned by absentee landlords. It was usual for the Church Vestry to appoint two able persons as Overseers of the Poor and in 1597 parishes were given authority to raise a Poor Rate to be used as follows:

1. Setting to work children of parents not thought fit to maintain them. Such children were often apprenticed.
2. Setting to work people with no means to maintain themselves and with no ordinary trade.
3. To provide a stock of materials for the poor to use.
4. For the relief of the old and impotent not able to work.

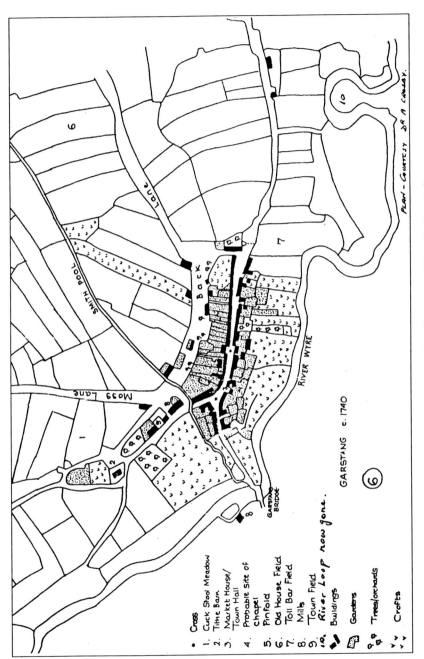

Plan of Garstang c. 1740. (Courtesy of Dr. A. Crosby)

• Cross
1. Cuck Stool Meadow
2. Tithe Barn
3. Market House/ Town Hall
4. Probable site of chapel
5. Pinfold
6. Old House Field
7. Toll Bar Field
8. Mills
9. Town Field
10. River Loop now gone.
■ Buildings
Gardens
Trees/orchards
Crofts

GARSTANG c. 1740

⑥

PLAN - COURTESY DR A CROSBY.

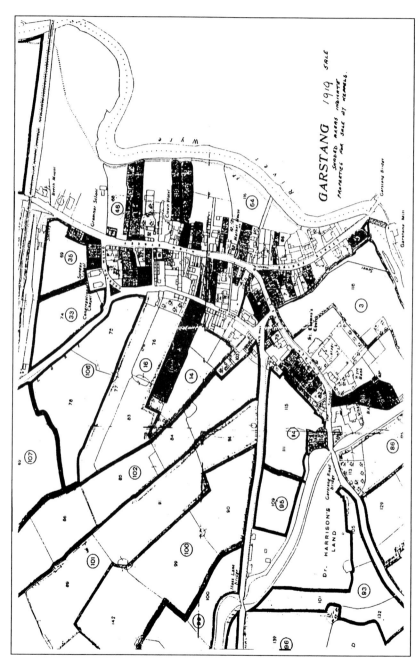

Plan of Garstang at the time of 1919. Sale of Town Properties

Bridge Street — Liberal Club on right

Bridge Street

Bridge Street — Golden Ball Inn on right

Church Street — Looking East, c. 1910

Church Street — Looking West, c. 1905

High Street — Looking North. Wards Temperance Hotel mid right

Lancaster Road — Looking North. Grammar School end facing

High Street — Looking South, c. 1890

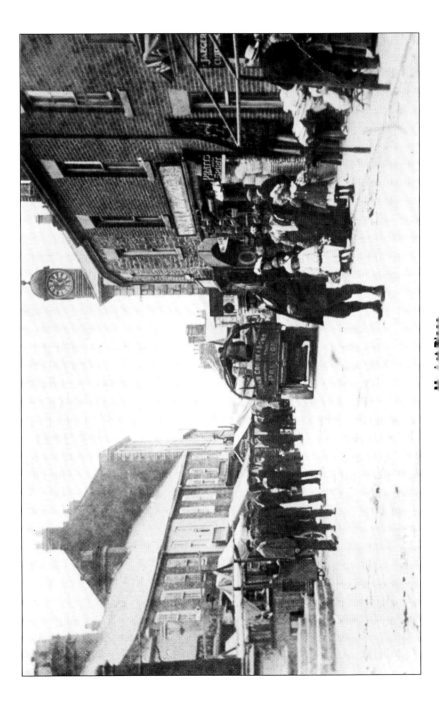

Cattle Fair, c. 1898

St. Thomas' School, Church Street c. 1905

Greenhalgh Castle, c. 1927

GARSTANG & KNOTT END RAILWAY

COCKERHAM MOSS

PILLING MOSS

RAWCLIFFE MOSS

Cockerham

Winmarleigh

NATEBY

Nateby Ho.

GARSTANG TOWN

Garstang & Catterall

Lancaster Canal

R.Wyre

A.6

B.5272

B.6430

A.588

B.5377

Stakepool

PILLING STATION

Carr Lane

Green Dick's Lane

Pilling Village

Lamb's Lane

PREESALL

KNOTT END

B.5270

B.5377

A.588

One mile

PLAN PRODUCED COURTESY LANCASTER MUSEUMS.

Garstang - Knott End Railway. (Courtesy of Lancaster Museums)

There is no doubt that the Church in Garstang, either through the Mother Church in Churchtown or the Chapel of Ease in Garstang, would have followed this pattern of Poor Relief.

Under the Poor Law Amendment Act of 1834 a Board of Guardians was appointed in Garstang, inter alia, to look after the Poor. The first meeting took place on 31st January 1838, when among other officials, the first Registrar of Births Marriages and Deaths was appointed. He controlled the first census in 1841 and received £53/18/2d. to cover fees and expenses. Garstang Guardians had the responsibility of appointing Medical Officers for the District and appear to have been in almost continuous dispute with these officers over pay and duties.

One of the aims of the 1834 Act was to discourage vagrancy. All able-bodied people were expected to look for work and those who would not, were sent to inhospitable workhouses. Relieving Officers appointed by the Guardians had authority to provide assistance. During the 1840's these payments in Garstang averaged about £120 per month.

There was already a Workhouse established in Stubbins Lane, Claughton, and in 1838 it was leased from Mr FitzHerbert Brockholes and became Garstang Workhouse. The workhouses were not supposed to be comfortable but this building in Stubbins Lane must have been awful. The Poor Law Commissioners wrote on several occasions to the Guardians requiring them to make improvements. The Guardians kept prevaricating until eventually the Commissioners, claiming that it was the worst Workhouse in Lancashire, save only Liverpool, said that if the Guardians did not rebuild they would take steps to have the present building closed and erect a new one, sending the Guardians the bill. This was in 1870 and even after this threat it was not until 1874 that the workhouse building was subsequently rebuilt on the site now occupied by The Beeches on Bowgreave. It was built as cheaply as possible and on the inside the bricks were not plastered, but lime-washed. There is a lot of information in the Minute Books about the running of the Workhouse.

Garstang Corporation

While the Select Vestry and the Guardians were looking after the health and welfare of the people of Garstang, there was another level of authority in the Town. Edward II had granted the Abbott of Cockersand the right to hold a weekly market. This would lapse with the dissolution of the monastery and there was probably no market in the town until 1597 when Elizabeth I renewed the grant of a market and two annual fairs in June and November. These rights were surrendered to Charles II and on the 5th August 1680 he granted a Charter of Incorporation to the town under which a Bailiff and 7 Burgesses were to be elected for life and could only be removed from office if they ceased to reside in the town, requested to vacate the office or committed some misdemeanour. The Bailiff was elected annually in November from among the Burgesses. Any vacancy was filled by the decision of the remainder.

There is little recorded evidence of the activities of the Bailiff and Burgesses. The Record Office features a book compiled in 1833 by T W Clarke containing some snippets of information. Viz: -

1. The Bailiff be allowed no more than £1/10/0d.
    expenses on the day of his election, and no more than
    6/8d expenses at each Fair (not including the wages of
    the Tollmen).

2. The Bailiff shall be allowed any sum, not exceeding 20/-
    in connection with his attending the Assizes or
    Quarterly sessions.

3. If the Bailiff dies in office, the Burgesses shall elect a successor for the remainder of his term.

4. The Bailiff shall have the right to appoint one Freeman during his term of office.

5. When elected Burgess, the new man shall be allowed 5/- expenses on that day, and the new Burgess shall become Bailiff in the next year. (It appears the Bailiff's job was not much sought after).

6. Entertainment expenses of the Bailiff on the day of election would only be paid if the entertainment was in Garstang.

7. A list of persons in Trade or Business in the town was to be kept, and all persons on that list would pay stallage (rent exacted for the privilege of erecting stalls) and piccage (money paid for preparing the ground on which booths were erected at fairs) unless excused.

8. Sons of freemen of the Borough were to be admitted as freemen and sworn against payment of 5/- to the Bailiff (for the use of the town), 2/6d to the Town Clerk and 1/- to the Town Sergeant.

9. Apprentices having served 7 years were admitted as Freemen against payment of 7/6d to the Bailiff, 2/6d. to the Town Clerk and 1/- to the Town Sergeant.

10. The Town Clerk was to be chosen by Bailiff and Burgesses.

11. The Town Sergeant was to be chosen by the Bailiff only and be discharged by him for failure to do his duties.

The first Town Hall was probably built just after 1680. It was damaged by fire in 1750 and rebuilt in 1755.

The chief concerns of the Bailiff and Burgesses appear to have been the running of the weekly market and the annual fairs. The control of the Grammar School, built in 1756, and the letting of the two shops in the Town Hall was also their responsibility. Although there is little evidence of their activities, the job of Burgess appears to have been something of a sinecure and an excuse to enjoy an occasional binge at the town's expense.

Some of the accounts of some of the Bailiffs are listed, and below are quoted individual items from these: —

1764	Received at Martinmas Fair	£4.14 . 2
	Half year's rent for 2 Town Hall shops	£1. 6 . 0
	Received from a Dancing Master at the Town Hall	17. 6
	Paid Schoolmaster 1 year's salary	£6.15. 0
	Bill for Sergeant's Cloak	£2. 6. 6
1729	Bailiff's expenses on election raised to	£2. 0. 0
1730	Given to poor disbanded sailors and soldiers	13. 0

1732	Visiting the Duchess of Hamilton (probably at Waddacre Hall)	5. 0
1754	Spent on removing the Old Cross	1. 8
1802	Bailiff's expenses on day of election raised to	£2.10. 0
1830	Proclaiming King William IV. Mr McKie's account (Royal Oak)	£4 .4.10
	12 other publicans' accounts. (This must have been quite a pub crawl)	£1.14.10
1831	Distributing coppers to the children at the Horse Fair	3. 0
1832	Cleaning Town Hall after ceiling fell in	1. 0

Every year the accounts of a number of publicans were settled. There are no accounts shown after 1846.

In 1822 it was agreed that a Town Seal be made depicting a Lyon Levant and the inscription "Ville de Garstang 1680". The original seal showed the Lyon facing left. Today's impressions have the Lyon facing right.

It was also agreed to have a stamp made for marking Weights and Measures. This bore the initials GR surmounted by a crown and on the left a Lyon Levant.

In 1843 the right of Garstang to mark the weights and measures of residents in the town was upheld after an incident in which a County Inspector seized various weights and measures from local hostelries claiming they were not properly stamped. The case ended up in court but was dismissed by the magistrates when the Bailiff produced evidence of the rights of the Town in this matter.

The Municipal Corporations Act of 1883 ended the authority of the Bailiff and Burgesses, when Garstang Rural District Council was formed.

Garstang Rural Sanitary Authority

Under the Public Health Act of 1872, Rural Sanitary Authorities were formed for the purpose of controlling the health, sewerage and draining of their areas, and of providing a supply of piped pure water. Members of the Authority were nominated. The Garstang Authority covered an area westward from Garstang to Pilling and northward to Ellel. This area was identical to the one subsequently covered by Garstang Rural District Council. The inaugural meeting was held on 23rd October 1873 with Mr William MacNeal in the chair. The clerk, on a salary of £20 per annum, was Mr Thomas Noble. A pencil note in the Minute Book states that he was appointed by Act of Parliament and commenced his duties on 29th August 1872. Mr Ambrose Fox was appointed Inspector of Nuisances on a salary of £70 p.a., a position he held until his retirement in 1891.

The only other paid officer was the Medical Officer, a job that was initially advertised with a salary of £50 p.a. This failed to attract applicants, as did an increased offer of £70 p.a. Finally it was advertised at £1/1/- per visit plus 6d a mile travelling expenses. Four people applied and a Mr B Denham was appointed on 18th December 1873, but on 2nd July 1874 he informed the Authority that he wanted to relinquish the post. No reason is given, but the fact that four doctors were subsequently appointed to cover the same area, at the same remuneration, suggests that Mr Denham may have found the distances he had to travel were too great. This state of affairs continued until

October 1877 when Dr Thomas J Irvine was appointed Medical Officer for the whole area at a payment of £1/1/- per visit, which was changed to a fixed salary of £50 p.a. in May 1880. He was replaced in 1882 by a Dr Fisher on the same salary, which continued until the Authority ceased to exist in 1894.

While the Inspector of Nuisances reported to each meeting of the Authority, little specific detail is given about the nature of the nuisances. In the main they appear to relate to dirt accumulating in drains, dirty water in wells, over-crowding of houses, poor accommodation and smells from various sources.

There were occasional outbursts of contagious diseases. In 1877 there were 6 cases of smallpox in Catterall, 2 in Nateby and 1 in Scorton. The Authority decided, at an Extraordinary General Meeting on 22nd March 1877, to provide free disinfectant to everyone to help combat the outbreak and also instructed that, when smallpox was diagnosed in a house, no one should leave or visit the premises – except presumably the doctor. It was also resolved that in the case of any further single outbreak of the disease the sufferer should be sent to Preston Fever Hospital. In the event of multiple cases in the same house, it was decided that they should all be taken to the Workhouse Fever Ward. In 1886 Preston Sanitary Authority said that, in view of their local need, they would not be able to take any further patients from the Garstang area into their Fever Hospital. It was at this time that Garstang first considered building one or more local hospitals.

In 1877 the Local Government Board produced model Bye Laws covering the cleansing of footways and pavements, the removal of house refuse, cleansing of earth closets, privies, ashpits and cesspools and also covering Common Lodging Houses. Following this, in February 1878, the Medical Officer and Inspector of Nuisances inspected the sanitary conditions of Garstang and reported that they were most unsatisfactory. There was no immediate rush to remedy the position but in December 1878 the Inspector produced a plan for the sewerage of Garstang, which it was resolved should be submitted to the ratepayers. The terms "drainage" and "sewerage" are very loosely used throughout the Minutes and it is not always possible to know whether sewers or drains are being referred to. However, there appeared little sense of urgency, as the above plan is not mentioned again.

In July 1880 the Inspector again reported the necessity for the drainage of the Town and it was agreed to form a Parochial Committee from the ratepayers of the Town to discuss the matter. In the meantime urgent work on the draining of Back Lane (Park Hill Road) was carried out by Collinson's at a cost of £29/10/-. In 1894 sewers were laid along the High Street and down Church Street connecting with Smithspool. In 1906 a major scheme to carry sewage from Garstang under the River Wyre to settlement tanks on the Bonds side of the river was proposed but the Minute Books do not record if this was done. There do not appear to be surviving plans of local sewers at that time.

As mentioned earlier, Model Bye Laws relating to the

cleaning of towns were published in 1877, but it was not until 1883 that the Authority asked the Inspector to produce a scheme for the regular cleaning of Garstang. This was to include a plan of all the watercourses, ash or other middens and refuse heaps that would have to be cleared. The job of scavenging was put out to tender annually, and apart from two years was done, not always efficiently, by Mr Robert Marsden at a price of £15 p.a. rising to £16 in 1887. He then offered to buy himself a cart to help do the job if he was given at least a 3-year contract. In 1891 he declined to do the work for £18 p.a. and Mr J Gardner took over on a £15 tender.

The first mention of the Authority concerning itself with street lighting occurs on 27th August 1878 when it was resolved to obtain tenders for the lighting of Garstang with oil lamps. Only two tenders were received, one of £11/10/- from Mr Thomas and the other of £10/10/- from Mr Storey. The latter was accepted and renewed the next year. However, an attempt to obtain the contract for a third year at an increased price of £12 was refused and a contract was given in November 1880 to the newly formed Garstang Gas Company who were to light the streets for a period of 5 years from 1st October to 31st March at a price of £17/10/- (£1/5/- per lamp). This indicates that a total of 14 lamps were sited around the town. In 1885 the contract was renewed on an annual basis of £1/7/6 per lamp. In 1891 a 7-year contract was signed at 30/- per lamp on the understanding that the two lamps in Bridge Street were moved to new positions, that an extra light was provided in Moss Lane plus a further one outside the Gas Works.

In October 1891 Mr Ambrose Fox, the Inspector of Nuisances, retired after 19 years service and applied to the Authority for an annuity of £25. For the next nine months the Authority, and presumably the townsfolk, seem to have been divided over whether or not any payment should be made. On two occasions proposals to make a payment were defeated. In both cases the decision was rescinded at subsequent meetings. A resolution was passed at a Ratepayers' Meeting requesting that favourable consideration be given to the request. The Local Government Board said £15 was a maximum that could be paid. Eventually a payment of £10/10/- p.a. was sanctioned.

During the early years of its existence the Authority financed expenditure by assessing the whole Rural District. In 1877 the rateable value of the Union was £86,979 and a 1d rate yielded £362/8/-. In 1881 it was decided to levy an extra rate on Garstang whenever exceptional expenditure in the town was needed. Subsequently in most half years a levy of between £25 and £50 was made. The rateable value of Garstang in 1887 was £3,204 and a 1d rate would yield £13/7/-.

On 11th August 1887 a resolution was passed proposing: "That a deputation be sent to the Meeting of Enquiry to be held that day at Garstang Town Hall under the Municipal Corporation Act 1883 respecting Garstang Corporation and that such deputation do express the opinion of the Sanitary Authority to the effect that they wish to disclaim the management of the property belonging to the late

Corporation and to recommend the appointment of local Trustees resident in the Township of Garstang for such purpose". There is no note of the outcome of that meeting, but on 11th January 1889 the Town Trust was formed to take over the properties owned by the Town.

The last meeting of the Authority was held on 27th December 1894 when the responsibilities of the Authority were taken over by Garstang Rural District Council, whose members were elected by ballot.

One could have hoped for more explicit Minutes of the activities of the Authority during its 21 years' existence. All one can say is that reading the Minutes one can sense the steady movement of life in the Town towards the 20th Century, while at the same time noting the extreme reluctance of our Victorian forbears to spend money.

Garstang Rural District Council

The Rural District Council was formed in 1894. All the Minute Books are available in the Records Office in Preston. In the early days, up to the outbreak of war in 1914, the main concerns of the Council, as regards Garstang, were sewerage, road usage and the building of a hospital.

There are many mentions of plans for sewerage work to be carried out in the town but, as before mentioned, it would appear to be about 1906 before a satisfactory system was established.

The arrival of the motor car was noted in Garstang by the granting, in 1898, of licences to store and sell petroleum to Joseph Hartley and James Storey. In 1899 Lancashire County Council turned down a request from the RDC that the recesses on the bridge over the River Wyre in Garstang be filled in, as they were being fouled. The LCC pointed out that the recesses were there as refuges for pedestrians.

Complaints are noted quite frequently about the dust caused by motor vehicles travelling on dry roads. On 25th October 1900 a letter was sent to the LCC drawing attention to the danger caused by motor cars travelling at high speed, and asking them to consider requiring all motor vehicles to be numbered clearly, so that owners could be identified. Again in 1903 support was given to a resolution passed by Pocklington RDC requiring all car drivers to be licensed, and such licence to be forfeited for at least

12 months if a driver was guilty of breaking the speed limit. A copy of this Resolution was sent to the Prime Minister, the local MP and the Local Government Board. Finally on 3rd May 1906 a Resolution passed by St Alban's RDC received unqualified support. After its adoption, a copy was sent to the local MP and the Local Government Board. This Resolution stated that:

"In the opinion of this Council the serious attention of HM Government should be drawn to the terrible nuisance of and damage caused by motor vehicles in this district. That this Council is of the opinion that all motor vehicles should be in some measure further taxed and that a grant from the revenue so derived should be made towards the expense of watering the roads in every District used by motor vehicles with a view to reducing the vexatious and damaging nuisance caused by the dust, the aforesaid damage and nuisance particularly affecting the farm crops for a considerable distance from such roads and also the properties immediately adjoining the roads. That the Council is of the opinion that the cost of preventing the damage so caused should not be borne by the local rates but by the owners of motor vehicles. Further that serious danger occurs to persons using the highways from motor vehicles raising such great clouds of dust as render the sight of other vehicles almost impossible to give time to get out of the way."

This problem of dust would not be solved until tarmacadam came into use after the 1914-18 war.

The attempt to build a local hospital is discussed in a later chapter, as are the problems concerning the bridge over the River Wyre at Hippingstones.

On 19th February 1903 an advert was placed in local
papers covering the job of Sanitary Inspector's Workman
whose duties would be:

1. To clean and examine the Sewage Works in the
   Workhouse Grounds twice daily including Sundays.
2. To clean and examine the Sewage Works at
   Bowgreave (South) at least once daily.
3. To clean and examine all other Sewage Works and
   Sewers at present laid, or to be laid and to carry out
   the Sanitary Inspector's instructions.
4. To cut trenches and lay any sanitary drains that may
   be required in the District.
5. To attend the laying of all new sewers which may be
   laid by the Council without contract and to make all
   joints of new pipes for all new drains and sewers in
   the district.
6. To keep in order the Bonds rubbish tip and any other
   tip that the Council may order.
7. When not employed as above to work on the
   Highways.

Note. Applicants must understand the work of tree
lopping. It will be necessary for the workman to have a
bicycle. Applicants to state wage required and enclose
two character testimonials.

Did he need a bike?

It was agreed in Council that no applicants asking for more than 25/- per week be considered. Over 50 applications were received, only 4 asking for 25/- or less. A James Ribchester of Garstang got the job at 25/- per week. I wonder how long he lasted?

The Council met initially in the Town Hall but in 1912 moved into the new Union Buildings erected on the High Street opposite the Grammar School.

The Rural District Council continued until 1974, when it was replaced by Wyre Borough Council.

The Parish (Town) Council.

In 1894 the Select Vestry was replaced by the Parish Council. The first six councillors were nominated, apparently by the members of the Select Vestry. At a meeting of Parochial Electors held on 17th March 1919 those present were asked to nominate and vote for six persons to become Councillors. This was the first occasion on which Councillors were actually elected.

Unfortunately Minute Books prior to 1910 appear to have been lost. Meetings do not always appear to have been well attended and on one occasion on 3rd July 1913 only the Clerk, Mr J B F Whiteside, was present. He read the Minutes of the last meeting and passed a resolution that the Lighting and Watching Act of 1833 be continued for another year and that a sum of £38/5/- be raised therefore. Presumably his action would have been approved later.

This book is only concerned with the development of Garstang up to the end of the 1914-18 War, but the Minute Books from then until today make interesting reading.

The Town Trust

The Corporation of Garstang was dissolved by the Municipal and Corporations Act of 1883, and Garstang became a Parish whose affairs were controlled by Garstang Rural District Council. The tangible assets of the Corporation were however not taken over by the Rural District Council. The Municipal Act of 1883 anticipated this situation and provided that all property and rights of a dissolved Corporation should be applied for the public benefit of the inhabitants and it was incumbent upon the Charity Commissioners to devise a scheme under which such property could be vested in a "body corporate". Garstang Town Trust was set up under such a scheme. Initially the Trust consisted of:

2 Ex-officio Trustees (The Guardians of the Poor)
4 Ratepayers selected by the Parish of Garstang, in vestry assembled
1 Representative from Lancashire and Cheshire Antiquarian Society
4 Co-optative Trustees, being persons residing or carrying on business in Garstang

The property controlled is the Town Hall, the Market Hall (since 1927), the Arts Centre (formerly the Grammar School) and the Market Cross (registered as an ancient monument). Other small artefacts include two Halberds and Staff, which are currently displayed in the Arts Centre.

The most important assets were the right to hold the

weekly street market and the annual fairs and to collect tolls from these events. The annual fairs ended when the Cattle Fair to be held in November 1933 was cancelled because of lack of support.

The Town Sergeant was appointed by the Town Trust. His duties were to act as Town Sergeant, Town Crier and official Bill Poster for the Town. He was required to keep the Town Hall and Market Hall clean and tidy and to prepare rooms for meetings. He was responsible for ensuring that market stalls were erected on Thursdays and Saturdays by 9 am. He had to collect the Tolls and pay these into the bank. Stalls had to be cleared by 9.30 pm. In the mid 1920's his wages were 16/- per week. The Town Trust provided a uniform for use on Market Days, Fair Days and Saturdays.

The early Minute Books of the Trust are missing but from 1911, when read in conjunction with the Town Council Minute Books, they give a good insight into the affairs and development of Garstang from the First World War to the present day.

The Grizedale Reservoirs

Fylde Water Works was formed in 1853 but did not become active until 1860. In that year a scheme was drawn up to provide water from the Grizedale stream, said to be the purest in the area, for use by the Fylde Coast towns. A reservoir was to be built at Grizedale, large enough to provide 750,000 gallons a day. By early 1863 the depth of the reservoir was 112 feet below the top bank and 40 feet below the bed of the stream, but the engineers were having problems finding a watertight bottom. They finally recommended that the bottom of the trench be lined with concrete to a level above where the spring waters were flowing in. Good quality puddle clay was to line the sides above the concrete level.

The work proved more difficult than anticipated and it was not until 16th November 1866 that the reservoir was reported full. It had cost £29,976/13/5. In June 1867 a leak was reported in the reservoir and the place where this was occurring was discovered 70 feet below the top bank. It was repaired by May 1869 at a cost of £4,159/11/5. In 1873 it was agreed to build Barnacre Reservoir near the site of Sconce Tarn. This was completed by 1875 and in 1876 it was decided to split this reservoir into two. The total cost of building these reservoirs was £47,071/10/-.

In December 1876 a new leak appeared in the Grizedale Reservoir and during the next two years attempts were made to solve the problem. It was discovered that one reason for the leak was that the layers of concrete used for repairs in 1868 had not bonded together, and water was seeping through the layers. In 1879 work stopped on seeking to repair Grizedale and it was not until 1881 that work recommenced and all the old puddle clay at the north end of the reservoir was removed. Repairs continued but it was October 1883 before this reservoir was reported full of water for the first time since 1876.

Repairs to this reservoir cost £39,804/2/6, far more than the initial cost of building. The bill included an amount of £8,037/15/- paid to Catterall Hall Works for water bought in to supplement that lost from Grizedale.

In 1897 an Act was passed transferring the assets of Fylde Water Works to a new Company called Fylde Water Board set up by Blackpool, Fleetwood, Lytham, St Annes and Kirkham Local Authorities.

In 1902 a new larger reservoir called Grizedale Lea was planned to be built on the northeast side of the existing Barnacre Reservoirs. Work was started in 1904. Lodging houses and a recreation room were built on the site to accommodate most of the 300 men employed on the job. It was finished in 1911 at a cost of approximately £100,000.

The capacity of the reservoirs at that time was: —

Grizedale	80,000,000 gallons
North and South Barnacre	15,600,000 gallons
Lea	33,200,000 gallons
Total	128,800,000 gallons

Garstang was supplied with water from this source in 1873 when a 4″ main was laid from Dimples Lane down to the Market Place and a 3″ main was laid down the streets.

Garstang Friendly Society — 1770 to 1824.

Friendly Societies were organizations formed initially around this time in towns to look after the welfare of workers.

The under-mentioned Articles and Minutes speak for themselves.

Articles and Orders

To be observed by a Society of different Trades and Artificers associated in the Town and Parish of Garstang for raising and supporting a Box or Fund of money for helping, relieving and assisting each other on just and proper occasions. For burying our dead and promoting peace, love and unity among ourselves.

Begun by 17 members on 13th February 1770

1. Officers –Two stewards and one clerk. A Box to be purchased to house books of records and cash. Four keys for the Box, one each held by the stewards and clerk, and one by the landlord of the House where the society meets.
2. Monthly meetings – 1st Wednesday in month – 7 pm to 9 pm.
   Each attender to spend 2d. If official is away (unless sick) he must send key and 2d. If he fails to send key he must pay 1/- or be excluded.
3. Officials shall only serve six months and members

shall hold office in turn until all have served, then the rota recommences. Any member refusing to serve will pay 5/- or be excluded.

4. People wishing to join will be vetted, and admitted at quarterly meetings. Members of other clubs will not be admitted.
5. 1/- entrance fee.
6. Members pay 1/- and spend 2d at each quarterly meeting. The 1/- to go in the Box and 2d to go to the club.
7. After two years as a member – if unable to work – stewards shall visit to check and then pay 5/- per week for 12 months, then 2/6 per week. If stewards fail to visit you, they must pay 2/6.
8. No benefit is payable if ill health is due to drink or debauchery. Members must be over 20 and under 40 when admitted unless a two-thirds majority of members consent.
9. Overseas journeys on business of less than one year and one day shall not disqualify. Arrears must be paid.
10. Anyone swearing at Club meetings – calling for drinks or tobacco without Steward's consent – or calling stewards or clerk by any other name than Steward or Clerk – fined 1d. Stewards are personally responsible if overspending occurs on Club nights.
11. No gambling or disputes or quarrels during Club meetings – fined 6d.
12. Any noisy person who refuses to keep quiet, or drunken person, during Club meetings – fined 2d.

13. Complaints between members settled by a Committee of Officers and six senior members. The parties have the right to object to two of the members. Refusal to accept judgment will merit a fine of 2/- or exclusion.
14. Every member must have paid all monies due by him to the Club on quarter day, or be excluded from the Club.
15. Stewards must render full accounts at the end of their term of office.
16. After two years membership, if a member dies, the sum of £1 is to be given to the person responsible for the funeral. All members, unless sick, must attend the funeral or pay 6d, which sum is to be given to the widow (if any), or put in the Box.
17. Members leaving town for one year or more must advise Stewards of new address or forfeit 6d.
18. On first Wednesday in New Year at 12 noon all members (except sick) shall meet and pay 1/- to buy moderate refreshments of meat and drink. (1/- fine if not present). All members to behave in an orderly fashion.
19. Stewards and Clerk have the power to move Box and Meeting to any Public House in Garstang.
20. Any member taken ill, whilst residing outside Garstang, shall on production of Certificate signed by Churchwardens of Town where he is residing, confirming sickness, receive payments to which he is entitled without need of a steward's visit. Money wrongly claimed to be repaid and member excluded.
21. Stewards finishing term of duty shall be "Auditors"

of Society's affairs for next six months. No money from the Box shall be spent other than for sick or death pay, and no money to be put out for interest or otherwise, except by majority vote at Quarterly meeting.

22. No one shall be excluded from membership – except underground workers. No non-member to enter Club Room on meeting night except to pay a member's arrears. Allowed one drink, then he must leave. Articles of the Society may be altered by majority vote – except for Article 19 – the Box must not be moved from Garstang.

Society Minutes

3rd October 1770

Clerk, who is to be a member paying usual dues, to be paid 6d per member (as a salary) at the yearly meeting. Every member shall, whether they attend or not, pay to the Landlord of the House where the Box is kept, at the yearly meeting, the sum of 8d. for eating and 6d for liquor. Each member of Society shall pay for a white rod to be provided by the Stewards at the first yearly meeting. After that they shall be Members of this Society, or be excluded from this Society, and that each member living in the parish of Garstang shall attend unless hindered by sickness at the House where the Box is kept by 10 o'clock in the forenoon, on every yearly meeting and walk in procession with the said rods from thence to the Chapel of Garstang. The Stewards, Clerk, two Overseers and

Landlord of the House first, and the rest of the members in Seniority of Entrance to join such procession or forfeit 1/- each to the Box or be excluded from the Society.

6th January 1773
Agreed that members who live a great distance from the place where the Box is kept may be excused serving as Stewards on payment of 2/6 into the Box.

5th January 1774
It is this day further agreed by a majority of the members that no member shall be admitted for the future unless he pays, over and above what is ordered by these Articles, the sum of 6d for each and every £5 that the stock shall exceed £20, and that all members that now do, or hereafter shall belong to this Society shall provide themselves with a black silk scarf, gloves and white ribbon to attend the funeral of every deceased member dying within the Parish of Garstang.

4th January 1775
No member who is above one quarter in arrears with payments to the Box shall be entitled to benefit.

6th January 1779
Resolved that every member living within five miles of the centre of Garstang shall attend the funeral of a deceased member, with their respective Rods, Scarves and Gloves, or shall pay 2/- into the Box. Stewards to notify members, and to be reimbursed not more than 1/- each (the Stewards) for expenses.

5th January 1780
Funeral allowance raised from 20/- to £2.

It is difficult to estimate from the accounts just how the Club flourished. Different stewards had their own book-keeping methods.

Subscriptions of 1/- per quarter are shown but no mention is made of the 2d per week members were supposed to pay. A limited amount is shown under "forfeits".

The membership appears initially to have been 30-40 members but in the early 1800's amounts shown as "Club Monies and Forfeits" vary each quarter. The first quarter's receipts averaged about £25 and the other three quarters approximately £7. It is impossible to deduce membership numbers from these figures.

Payments out:

1809 £30/5/-
1814 £75/0/-
1818 £69/1/-
1823 £48/10/-
1824 £61/5/-
1806 £28/8/-
1791 Maximum of 7/- per week sick pay appears to have commenced.
1808 Funds built up to a balance of £313/2/11 then declined steadily.
1823 £30 lost when A. Worswick (Bank) went bankrupt. (Three dividends paid - £7/15/1, £4/5/3 and £2/2/7).

1824 Affairs of the society were suspended.

1846 On 19th December a distribution was made of 3/- per head to surviving members or deserving relatives — 40 at 3/- = £6/0/0. The amount of money in the Box was £6/8/11½d. Balance distributed; 2 at 3/- , 1 at 2 /11½d. Also in Box – four Silk Scarves – one belonging to Thomas Wood was given to him – the others to Hugh Sowerbutts, the widow of Robert Gardner and the widow of William Holden.

1847 On 1st March a Colour Belt and Locket were sold for 1/- and the Club Box was sold for 5/-. The sum of 6/- was given to the orphan children of John Dunderdale and Christopher Martin, former Club members.

I wonder what became of the Box!

Letter in Minute Book of Garstang Friendly Society

20th July 1867

Dear Friend

I wish to inform you I read your letter and have "examined" the contents – it informs me it is your intention to add 5s. to my rent – which I think is a good deal "to" much. You must consider we cannot make as much of our land as you do in London. We have very bad times here and in the neighbourhood of Garstang – I am sorry to say, a great deal worse till I ever knew them. I have lived in Garstang nearly 4 score years – I am old and scarcely able to earn a livelihood. I must say me and my parents have lived under Mr Cappels' family near 1 hundred years and I have never left them 1/- in arrears. I do not like to be turned out of doors on the Town so I must comply to your Demand – the land I occupy is not worth the money you value it.

I remain

Yours one of the oldest (family?) in the Town

G. Benson

N. B. James Benson's child was a person who received 3/- from the Friendly Society's Distribution.

Hippingstones Ford (Wyre Lane)

In September 1876 it was reported that the footbridge over the River Wyre at Hippingstones was in a bad state and dangerous. The Highways Board were advised by Counsel that it was not their responsibility. Although mention is made in Minutes that the bridge was regarded as unsafe there were apparently no developments until 1882 when Mr Fare, the agent of Lord Bective (land owner), wrote to the Highways Board drawing attention to the poor state of the bridge. It was resolved that the matter be left in abeyance. Later in the year Mr Fare wrote again saying that Lord Bective was prepared to put the bridge in a state of good repair if the Highways Board would then take over the responsibility for the maintenance. This offer was declined.

In February 1884 the Board agreed to discuss the matter with Mr Fare. Some consideration was given to the erection of a wood and iron bridge but eventually in May 1885 the Board decided to bear no part of the costs of the erection of a new bridge.

In June and July 1887 deputations of Ratepayers expressed the great inconvenience to the public at large of the absence of a footbridge at Hippingstones and urged the Board to erect one. Lord Bective again offered assistance. The Board again refused to act and when the matter was raised again in September 1889 it was resolved that nothing be done for 6 months.

In March 1895 the duties of the Highway Board were

taken over by the new Garstang Rural District Council. In October 1895 a deputation from Barnacre Parish Council and Garstang RDC met members of Lancashire County Council to discuss the erection of a bridge over the River Wyre at the Hippingstones Ford. A verbal report back to Garstang RDC advised that the LCC did not feel able to move in this matter. Nothing more is mentioned until 15th March 1900 when a simple entry in the Minutes states that the Council approved the erection of a bridge.

In 1908 the RDC received a letter from a joint meeting of Garstang and Barnacre Parish Councils asking for a bridge at Hippingstones. The RDC said they would be prepared to consider this if the Parish Councils would advise them what amount could be obtained from voluntary subscriptions towards the cost. The County Council was asked how much they would contribute and to advise on the cost of a ferro-concrete bridge.

The LCC advised that the cost of a bridge would be £1,950 and road diversions work would cost £400. They asked how many people would use the bridge. This estimate appears to suggest that a bridge taking vehicles should be built. Although the proposed site is not specified, it was probably intended to cross the river at the point where the ford leaves it on the eastern side, with a new piece of road linking up with Wyre Lane.

The local parishes thought this cost was too high and suggested estimates be obtained for the erection of a cart bridge and wooden footbridge on the site of the existing footbridge. In January 1910 the RDC resolved that the erection of a new bridge be deferred. In December of that year Barnacre Parish Council raised the subject again. They sent a letter, supported by affidavits, claiming that the footpath crossing the River Wyre at Hippingstones leading to Woodacre Hall had been used since before 1835. They asked the Council to take over the path as repairable by the public at large.   A Committee was appointed to look into the matter.

In March 1911 Garstang Parish Council wrote to the RDC asking for the erection of a footbridge over the Wyre at Hippingstones. After further correspondence the RDC resolved in January 1912 that they would take over the maintenance of the footpath to Woodacre if Garstang and Barnacre Parish Councils would contribute a reasonable amount towards the cost of the footbridge.

In October 1912 the Surveyor presented two estimates for the cost of erecting a wooden footbridge. A bridge 1ft wide would cost £85; a bridge 2ft wide £98. These estimates included the cost of erecting two central supports set in concrete in the river and the erection of a brick abutment on the Garstang side. Negotiations between the RDC and the Parish Councils took place during 1913 about who was to finance the bridge. Eventually the Local Government Board intervened and said that if the RDC would agree to strengthen the proposed bridge (cost additional £5) they would authorise Garstang and Barnacre Parishes to each pay £20 towards the cost.

In February 1914 it was reported that in a recent flood the water was 3ft over the bridge abutment. It was agreed that the new bridge should be 3ft 6" higher than the present abutment. The extra work would cost a further £28/12/- making a total of £99/17/-.

On 12th November 1914 it was reported that the bridge, built by Exors of R Hall of Forton, was complete. In March 1918 concrete was laid around the centre pillar to strengthen the support.

The Hospital Garstang Nearly Had

In 1886 Garstang Rural District Sanitary Authority resolved that one or more Cottage Hospitals should be built to care for infectious cases of sickness in the area. A suggestion was made that the Infirmary at the Workhouse in Bowgreave should be used, but this idea does not appear to have been followed up and there is no further mention of a Hospital in the Authority's Minutes until December 1892.

At that time Preston Infirmary advised that they would no longer admit cases of smallpox to the hospital from outside the Borough of Preston. In a newspaper article at that time Garstang Sanitary Authority were strongly condemned for not providing its own Isolation Accommodation.

In May 1893 the Authority again resolved that a permanent hospital for infectious diseases be erected in the area. A suggestion that a hospital be built on land owned by the Guardians adjacent to the Workhouse was rejected because the site was considered unsuitable. The Sanitary Authority ceased to exist in 1894 when its functions were taken over by the newly formed Garstang RDC. For the next few years any house in which someone was suffering from an infectious disease was designated a Temporary Hospital and was controlled by the Medical Officer for Health. In December 1906 a small committee was appointed to look for a convenient site on which to erect a 12-bed hospital with an administration block. The committee came up with a proposal to build such a hospital of corrugated iron on brick foundations. The full Council rejected their idea and referred the matter back to the committee who suggested they again look at the possibility of building near the Workhouse in Bowgreave. The Council rejected this and suggested that the committee look into the possible purchase of a portable hospital.

Nothing materialised and eventually the matter was shelved until after the local elections in June 1907. The newly elected Council approved the scheme proposed in 1906 for a 12-bed hospital and the committee was authorised to look for a convenient plot of land to be purchased. Several sites offered by local landowners were considered and rejected for various reasons. Other sites suggested by the committee were not available. Land at Nateby, on the A6 near Cross House, on Byerworth Lane and near Shepherds Farm were all considered. Eventually Mr Ormerod offered to sell land at Cabus (Ordnance Survey Field 163) on the right-hand side of the road to Lancaster and this was bought on 12th November 1908 for £550.

In May 1909 a quotation was obtained from Fylde Water Board of £180 to lay a 3 inch iron pipe water main from Manor Farm to the field gate and £90 for a 1 inch lead service main over the same distance.

A letter from the County Medical Officer suggested that the Council should erect:
- a pavilion for scarlet fever with 12 beds, a small observation pavilion with two separate wards, each

with 2 beds, so that cases of diphtheria could be treated. The pavilion might be built of corrugated iron with brick foundations.

- An administration block with wash-house, disinfecting chamber and other offices should be permanent erections.

A committee was appointed to fix the site for the buildings, then to draw up plans for carriageways and sewers. In October 1909 the committee recommended that the field should be drained and the hospital built on the highest point facing south.

In the Spring of 1910 it was resolved to ask Fylde Water Board to lay a 2-inch iron water main with hydrants in the field in lieu of a lead pipe. It was also decided to seek estimates for a hospital of brick construction with 2 wards of 6 beds each, 2 observation wards and an administration block all of best ordinary brick with slate roofs. Floors were to be either boarded or woodblocks on concrete.

In November 1911 estimates were received for £1,424 for a brick built hospital and £1,009/17/- for one constructed with wood and iron. The estimated cost of the carriageway, water main, ambulance and furnishings was £366/12/-.

In December 1911 the County Medical Officer suggested that the number of beds be reduced from 12 to 8 and advised various other amendments which were accepted in principle. The Hospital Committee agreed to the amendments and asked the Clerk to the Council to advertise for tenders to carry out the work. Separate estimates were obtained for each aspect of the work, including one for the plumbing, glazing and painting (£280/11/-) from R W Lang of Garstang. The total of the lowest estimates came to £1,580 for the buildings, which was in excess of the original estimated cost of the work. While the Committee agreed to accept the tenders the full Council refused and referred the matter back.

Nothing further appears to have happened until May 1913 when the Committee decided to obtain fresh tenders for the work. There is no evidence that these were ever received. In 1916 the field was let on an annual basis to a Mr Melling and in 1918 he was given permission to plough the field. Despite ten years of deliberations on the part of the Hospital Committee, no hospital was built in Garstang. Had it not been for the outbreak of World War 1, the outcome might have been different. Wyre Borough Council still owns the Hospital Field!

Printed by:
COLIN CROSS PRINTERS,
GARSTANG